ISBN: 978-1-953867-02-5

For Tony.

Thank you for loving me "as is," even though I come with a "no returns" policy.

Version 1.0. Created October 17th, 2020 Copyright ©2020. Updated March 2026
Julie Coraccio, Reawaken Your Brilliance, LLC, *Got Clutter?*
Series created March 20th, 2019.

Disclaimer and Terms of Use: The Author and Publisher have strived to be as complete as possible in the creation of this journal prompt book, contrary to the interpretation of the subject matter herein. Like anything else in life, there are no guarantees of success. Readers are cautioned to rely on their own judgment about their individual circumstances and to act accordingly. This journal may bring up strong emotions or uncover buried trauma. If a question is too difficult, put it aside until you feel more comfortable with the material. Have a support system in place and seek professional help if necessary.

This journal is not intended for use as a source of psychological, counseling, legal, business, or financial advice. All readers are advised to seek the services of competent professionals in these areas.

INTRODUCTION

In my work as a transformational, holistic coach and professional life organizer, I view myself as a mirror. I reflect my clients' inner clutter. Many times, clutter blocks deeper meaning. I view my job as supporting people to unearth their personal guidance to clear their clutter. Each of you reading and answering questions in this journal knows what's best for you, and your intuition/instinct/gut reaction is your best guide.

I have witnessed that when people clear physical clutter, inner clutter (emotional, mental, and spiritual) is released. Likewise, when clients remove inner clutter, they begin to remove physical clutter. When you let go of what no longer serves you, you can create the life you choose, deserve, and desire.

The purpose of this journal prompts workbook is to help you remove financial clutter from your life. Journaling can often cut to the chase and allow your inner wisdom to emerge. Journaling also helps you relax and find peace.

There are 365 questions in this workbook, and I provided a prompt a day for an entire year (you get a one-day break if you start in a Leap Year) to cover a wide variety of questions. You may be really motivated and answer all queries in a month, or it may take you an entire year, or longer, to complete. The prompts aren't numbered or dated, so you can go at your own pace. Don't focus on the number of questions and completing them all. Instead, put your energy into answering what you are able. Some prompts may be relevant; some might not apply to you at all.

The questions in this book focus on where I've seen many people, myself included, struggle. They serve to build a strong foundation for releasing financial clutter. While there are definitely more questions you could ask, these prompts will increase your awareness and enable you to move forward if you choose.

Finally, the journal includes a *Take Action* plan and an *Immediate Take Action* worksheet. Awareness + Action = Change. What you discover when answering these questions can motivate you to initiate clearing your clutter and change your life.

YOU'VE GOT THIS!

If you have had clutter for a long time, chances are you are feeling overwhelmed, anxious, or even scared. Please remember that you are not alone. You may have had friends, family, a coach, or even a professional organizer judge your clutter and/or embarrass you. No matter what happened in the past, try to leave those unpleasant experiences behind and be present. The present moment is your point of power to change.

Know that you can do this. Even if you've never cleared your clutter or done any self-examination, it's within your abilities. So many times, you sell yourself short and underestimate what you can accomplish. Whether it takes you one month, six months, one year, or longer to answer these questions, congratulate yourself for taking the first step to forge ahead in releasing financial clutter from your life.

You can keep this workbook private; you don't have to share your answers with anybody. However, it may help to share with a trusted friend, coach, therapist, or professional life organizer. Choose what feels right for you *right now*. It's okay to change your mind at any time.

Practice deep breathing and take breaks when you need. Honor your pace and don't set yourself up with unrealistic timetables. Commit to taking a step forward in some way every day—no matter how small. If you commit to answering the questions and creating a *Take Action* plan, you'll change your life. Little steps add up to big wins.

I encourage you to remember you are "perfect" as an "imperfect" you. Doing this workbook is about progress, not perfection. I used to think that there was some final destination I was supposed to reach. I wasn't sure what it looked like, where or what it was, or when I'd reach it, but I believed it was out there. I no longer take that view. Life is about learning, living, loving, and experiencing. It's about growing and becoming more of who you're meant to be.

On the next page is a pledge, and I hope you'll review it, sign it, and honor it. Be your own best friend, not your own worst enemy. Know that I'm cheering you on because I know you've got this!

When you clear your clutter, you can share your gifts with the world. You have important talents, and the world needs them now more than ever. Don't let clutter hold you back.

PLEDGE

I encourage you to customize or create a similar agreement and sign below.

I______________________, promise myself that I am doing my best to be fully present during this process. With purpose and honesty, I am reading and answering the questions in this workbook. This process might bring up uncomfortable issues and emotions. I am addressing my feelings the best I can and will seek professional support if necessary. I commit myself to taking action to declutter my life with clarity and determination. I am working to create a vision for my home and/or life that I choose, deserve, and desire.

I pledge:

- I am committed to clearing my financial clutter.
- I am honoring my pace and trusting the process.
- I am showing myself kindness and treating myself with respect.
- I am appreciating all that I am in each moment.
- I am consciously positive and support myself as I transform my life.
- I am surrounding myself with only supportive people during this process.
- I am focusing on the present.
- I am taking care of myself physically, emotionally, mentally, and spiritually to the best of my ability.
- I am seeking outside support, as I need it.
- I am finding positive ways of handling stress/problems/challenges other than shopping or engaging in other negative behaviors.
- I am prioritizing healing myself, decluttering, and taking action.
- I am acknowledging, honoring myself, and rewarding myself in healthy ways.
- I am good enough, worthy, and loved, no matter what.

Additionally:

Signature:
Date:

Awareness

+

Action

=

Change

HOW TO USE THIS JOURNAL PROMPT WORKBOOK

This journal contains questions I've found beneficial to people looking to clear financial clutter. While there are small groupings of questions, I purposely didn't separate even smaller subsections. (For example, budgeting, debt, and investing.) I kept this workbook structure loose, and I believe more subsections would stop the flow of answering questions.

No matter what, reading this journal prompt workbook and answering these questions adds to your self-knowledge. You might discover elements that will help you with your perspective, self-care, and self-kindness. You might even have an epiphany or two along the way. But to truly get the full benefit of this book, I highly encourage you to create a strategy with concrete steps to remove financial clutter. If you read the book and don't do anything, your life won't change. I want your life to change; that's why I wrote this book! When you clear your clutter, you can share your gifts with the world. I'd love to live in a world where everyone is sharing their gifts. Wouldn't you?

Remember, this is *your* journal, and there are no right or wrong answers. I encourage you not to get caught up in or feel frustrated if you're unsure how to answer a question. Ask your inner wisdom and voice for guidance, and trust that your soul is sharing with you what you need to know *right now*. Life isn't stagnant, so your answers may change in the future. The answers must come from you, and I wanted to provide as little influence as possible. You have all the answers within, and this workbook supports you to bring your wisdom to the surface.

My recommendation is to block out time to answer the questions thoughtfully. Do this when you have energy, can easily focus, and don't feel rushed. If you do when you're tired or when you can't concentrate, your mind may go on autopilot, and fresh answers might be more challenging to come by.

Sit where it's quiet, and you can be uninterrupted. If you're struggling, close your eyes to focus. Don't censor yourself; let the answers flow. You can go back through and clarify later. If you're feeling really stuck, refer back to the sections on your motivations and what clutter is costing you, as sometimes that can prompt an answer.

Now is not the time to worry about spelling and grammar. Run-on sentences, fragments, sound bites, and one-word answers are okay. What's important is getting your thoughts on paper. Go as in-depth as you are able. This is about what you're feeling, believing, sensing, and thinking, not sentence structure. You can use the whole page or keep it short.

On each page with a prompt and *Take Action*, there are two columns, one small and one big, separated by a line with a lotus symbol at the end. After you free write in the larger column, you have the option to come back and highlight what you found to be most valuable and write that in the smaller column. You don't have to take this additional step, but it makes it more manageable to create change. When you break chores into smaller steps, it not only makes you more likely to finish your to-do list but also gives you a sense of accomplishment and can help keep you motivated.

With the pertinent information in the smaller column, you can easily access your most valuable insights. You'll have teased out what was most important for you to know and do from answering the individual question. You can then use your smaller column insights more completely when you work on your *Take Action* plan.

I always recommend going with your intuition/gut instinct/first response. It's my experience that when someone says their gut instinct was "wrong," that they were listening to their ego, not their soul. If you prefer to think through the questions, consider your usual behavior or how you'd typically respond. What's most important is that you answer honestly so your responses support you in decluttering.

Honor your pace and commit to spending time on this! Add working on your journal prompts to your daily to-do list or make this a weekend exercise.

Have a self-care strategy in place. Sometimes, examining your financial clutter can bring up strong emotions or memories. Consider asking a friend to be available for support or having a coach or therapist that you can talk to if necessary.

You'll find *Take Action* pages after the questions at the end of the prompts. You can write any questions that may have come up and answer them. Jot down any other feelings, thoughts, or ideas. Record the actions you need to take to release your clutter.

WHY AM I MOTIVATED TO CLEAR CLUTTER?

Why did you buy this journal prompt book? Are you overwhelmed with credit card debt? Do you feel you're behind on saving for retirement? Have you developed poor spending habits? Are your finances causing you stress and worry?

Record your motivations to release financial clutter and how your clutter makes you feel. Also, document how you hope your life will improve when you release your clutter. Take the time to really answer these questions. By building a strong foundation of motivation, you'll support yourself when you become challenged or feel like giving up.

Review your inspirations when you're struggling to answer a prompt or feeling overwhelmed in creating your *Take Action* strategy.

Here are some examples:

My spending is out of control. I'm not sure why. I keep saying I'll stop, but then I can't. I always feel better after spending. I sell most of it, but that takes time and energy. My friends have started to notice, too, and think I'm super wealthy and want me to pay for stuff now. I'd like to feel in control of shopping. I want to get to the root of why I buy all the time, so I can release it and my angst. I'd like to be relaxed and feel joy naturally instead of trying to buy it.

All of our stuff causes my spouse and me to argue, and it raises my blood pressure. Our junk is everywhere! We buy and then don't use stuff. It's making me lose my mind as we have debt, which adds to my stress, which adds to my insomnia, which makes me exhausted and not exercise or eat well. I want us to use what we want or let it go. I want to be able to sleep, exercise, and eat well regularly. I want a clean home and no arguing.

I'm super worried about retirement as 50 is coming way too fast for me. I didn't handle my finances well when I divorced, and I'm not sure what to do. I'm so overwhelmed, I freeze. My parents weren't good with money, and I saw how they struggled when they were older. I don't want that for me. I want to feel not tired all the time with worry and anxiety. I'm going to be on the streets when I'm 70. I'd like to learn how to save, budget, and have money for the things I want. I don't live high off the hog, but I don't want to pinch every penny. I want to be less stressed and have more peace of mind.

Feel free to come back and add to this list at any time. The more reasons and details you write, the more motivation you'll have to release your clutter.

What's my financial clutter?

How does this clutter make me feel?

How can my life improve once I declutter?

WHAT'S CLUTTER COSTING ME?

Have you really, truly thought about what your financial clutter costs you? Do you experience insomnia because you're concerned about money? Are you frustrated because you haven't been able to save for a rainy day? Has your credit score cost you money with a higher interest rate? Does your family express concern over your spending habits?

Clutter affects peace of mind, increases stress, reduces quality of life, influences your relationships, costs time and money, and more. By writing down the real cost of your financial clutter, you can use your answers to inspire you, especially when you feel stuck. Be as specific as you're able to when writing your thoughts.

Record what clutter is costing you, and how what you're losing makes you feel. Also, document what you'll gain after decluttering. Honestly answer these questions. By understanding the true cost of your financial clutter, you can overcome your reluctance to let go of what no longer serves you.

Review what you are losing when you're struggling to answer a prompt or feeling overwhelmed in doing your *Take Action* plan. Here are some examples:

I keep stuffing my mouth with food because I'm so stressed and overwhelmed by my debt. Instead of expressing how scared I am, I eat. I never made the connection until now that my financial clutter is costing me my health. I'd like to feel financially free, at peace, and healthy.

My mother had a stroke 2 years ago, and it cost me $2,500 with a last-minute plane ticket, car rental, hotel, etc. I didn't have an emergency savings and put it all on my credit card. I was so angry that I didn't have cash socked away and had to pay interest. I want to build my savings and not have to worry if an emergency comes along. I want to feel confident I can handle what life throws at me and not always worry about money.

I need to invest and make my money work for me. I make a good living, but I want to be able to retire early and focus on my passion for painting. I don't know much and am worried someone will rip me off. I want to feel satisfied that I'm working towards my dream.

Write down what comes to you immediately. Feel free to add to your list as you work through the questions in the workbook.

My financial clutter is costing me:

1.

2.

3.

4.

5.

6.

7.

8.

9.

10.

What I'm losing because of this clutter makes me feel:

1.

2.

3.

4.

5.

6.

7.

8.

9.

10.

What I hope to gain when I declutter:

1.

2.

3.

4.

5.

6.

7.

8.

9.

10.

TAKE ACTION

When you write things down, you're more likely to complete your tasks.

You can read all the books in the library, listen to world-renowned healers, follow all the gurus on social media, and participate in numerous retreats, but if you don't do the work, your life will never change.

I encourage you to create a strategy to clear clutter from your life. When you were reviewing your answers, what resonated with you? Was there a question that sparked a realization or motivated you to remove clutter right away? What can you reasonably accomplish in a daily or weekly practice? What's feasible given your lifestyle and commitments? What other questions would you like to contemplate? These are just a few of the considerations that can help in creating strategies to clear your clutter.

You can start to declutter your finances immediately, or wait until you've completed this journal. You may decide to use this book as a companion guide to support you as you begin clearing clutter. Do what works for you and honor your pace, but I encourage you to *do something*!

Once you've completed a section or the book, take time to develop your *Take Action* plans. Without taking steps to move forward, your discoveries and moments of clarity won't make much difference.

Here are a few strategies when creating steps to clear your clutter:

- *Make SMART (specific, measurable, achievable, relevant, and time-bound) goals.* The more specific and realistic your goal, the more likely you'll achieve it. For example, I will save $20 a week. I will spend 15 minutes each day learning how to invest.
- *Keep it real.* Rome wasn't built in a day, but you can probably create a budget in one. Tackle no more than one or two items, as some habits are challenging to change. Set a date to check your progress.
- *Show yourself compassion.* If you committed to not spending money and buy a new outfit, don't beat yourself up. Get back on the horse and recommit to moving forward.
- *Be accountable.* How will you track your progress? Can you share what you're doing with a trusted friend? Use an app? When you're challenged, how will you remain motivated?
- *Find support.* How can you gain help and wisdom from others? Seek feedback from someone who has accomplished the same goal? Work with a friend or join

a group? If you remain stuck, what professional guidance and support can you use?

- *Go with the flow.* Life happens; small steps count. If you tend to hit the snooze button and miss your financial literacy group, can you find a night meeting? You can always amend your goals.
- *Staying the course.* Whether you make changes right away or it takes a year, remaining positive and keeping focused on your goal is an accomplishment.
- *Celebrate your progress.* Practice enjoying your personal growth and development, and reward yourself in healthy ways.

People with a lot of clutter tend to find it difficult to make decisions. Arriving at decisions often means making choices. The good news is that you can learn how to make choices. My nickname in college was "Indecisive One," yet the steps I've taken to declutter my life now make it easier to make decisions. If I can learn how to, you can too! Here are some tips for decision-making:

- Go with your gut response or intuition. It's there for a reason!
- Set standards: "I'll make a decision once I know A, B, and C." Once you have answers, make a choice.
- Consult a friend who has been through the same issue.
- Ask yourself if the decision is really meaningful. Will it matter a day, week, month, or year from now? If not, make a judgment or flip a coin.
- Make a list of the pros and cons. Prioritize which considerations are most important to you.
- Set a deadline to research facts and information to assess your options.
- Brainstorm and come up with several choices. Determine if the options are compatible with your values, interests, and abilities.
- Refer back to your priorities to guide you.
- Weigh possible outcomes. What's the worst that can happen? What will happen if you do A, B, or C? Can you live with the consequences?
- Establish a deadline to make a final decision.

I also encourage you to create an *Immediate Take Action* plan. You may have several items you need to address. Review your *Take Action* plan and pick no more than three items to complete *right now.* Focus on a few of your changes to implement, and before you know it, you'll have made real progress.

I'm relying on you to pace yourself according to your circumstances. If you need more guidance in dealing with what you discover, are challenged, or feeling paralyzed and stuck, consider hiring a coach, therapist, or professional organizer. You can also ask a trusted, non-judgmental friend or family member for support.

I'll provide a brief explanation of financial clutter and examples of how you might answer some questions. After the journal prompt queries, you'll find your *Take Action* plan. I provide guidance on creating a plan. Finally, there is the optional *Immediate Take Action* plan, which includes instructions.

The journey of clearing your clutter begins with one step.

Your self-worth isn't related to your net-worth.

Financial clutter can include credit card debt, minimal savings, and failing to plan for retirement. When you have financial clutter, it can affect all areas of your life. You can create mental clutter when you have anxiety from financial challenges. Regularly fighting with your spouse over finances leads to relationship clutter. You can create health clutter when your stress manifests into high blood pressure, insomnia, poor eating habits, etc.

When you're overwhelmed by money clutter, you can create physical clutter (buying things you don't need), emotional clutter (feeling shame because of finances), and spiritual clutter (not pursuing your passions because of a lack of funds).

Research has shown that debt and money challenges have real consequences for your health. Financial challenges can increase stress, cause fear and panic, and lead to depression.

Financial clutter may be an unusual concept for some, so I've devised queries for you to see what is perhaps invisible clutter in your life. I grouped similar questions to see how financial clutter can impact all areas of your life. Some prompts may not make sense right now, and the best move is not to answer. Revisit questions at a later date, as your circumstances change, and/or as the questions become valid.

EXAMPLES

Remember, all of your answers are valid. The words in bold represent what you might find as the most important part of your answers and are what you'd write in your smaller column.

What's my financial clutter kryptonite?

Shoes! Clothes! Accessories! I've taken over the master closet and all the other bedroom closets. It's this **vicious cycle** that I'm in. I **see something and have to buy** it. All my **girlfriends** spend a lot and I think that's part of it. I **find myself just going along** instead of saying, "**I already own enough!**" I **really want a romantic relationship**, but who'd want to date someone who is **in debt because of spending?** I want to **fall in love** not eat myself to death. I **need professional help to stop spending and figure out why I'm spending**.

Shoes! Clothes! Accessories! Vicious cycle. See something and have to buy. Girlfriends. Find myself just going along. I already own enough! Really want a romantic relationship. In debt because of spending. Need professional help to stop spending and figure out why I'm spending.

How does my financial clutter affect my mental state?

My **parents died poor**. **I paid for their funerals**. I have **not saved for retirement**. I am **scared to death** of not having enough money when I'm older. What if I need long term care? I have **insomnia** and **constantly worry**. I want to be able to **afford good health care**. I need to **hire a financial planner** and learn how to make my **money work for me.** Tomorrow I'm **asking HR about my benefits.**

Parents died poor. I paid for their funerals. Not saved for retirement. Scared to death. Insomnia. Constantly worry. Afford good health care. Hire a financial planner. Money work for me. Asking HR about my benefits.

What financial clutter makes me feel ashamed?

Hands down my **student debt**. I am **still paying** it off. I got a **bad deal** and I'm still **angry**. I feel like I'll **never get out from underneath** this. **I'm smart.** How can I have been so stupid? **I'm jealous.** I see all **my friends** with a nice homes, cars, vacations...**all my extra money goes to my debt.** I need to **confide** in someone because it's started to **affect my health**. Going to **reach out to my BFF**. She's **never judgmental** & **I need help** figuring out next steps.

Student debt. Still paying. Bad deal. Angry. Never get out from underneath. I'm smart. I'm jealous of my friends. All my extra money goes to my debt. Confide. Affect my health. Reach out my BFF. Never judgmental. I need help.

Ready to begin your prompts to release financial clutter?

What do I consider financial clutter?

What's my money clutter kryptonite (overspending, online shopping, late payments, etc.)?

Why haven't I stopped my clutter kryptonite?

What money concerns do I have *right now*?

Why is this a concern?

What action can I take *right now* (pay a bill, budget, etc.)?

Describe what a healthy financial lifestyle looks and feels like.

How can I best support myself (talk to a pro, read a book, listen to a podcast) for financial success?

How do my finances prevent me from creating a home and life I love?

What is my framework for making decisions about my finances?

What questions can help me refine or create my framework?

If all my financial needs were met tomorrow, what work or activities would I still do?

When I look back in 20 years, what would be the one thing I'd regret *not* supporting or funding?

What am I willing to sacrifice today to ensure a specific future outcome?

When does an extra dollar of wealth become less valuable to me than an extra hour of free time?

If I were no longer here, what is the one problem that would go unsolved because my support disappeared?

If I could live three different versions of my life, what would each look like: adventurous, work-focused, and service-oriented?

Which elements can I fund *right now*?

If I could leave my heirs only one principle instead of a portfolio, what would that be?

Does my current spending and gifting reflect that principle?

What does "enough" look like for my lifestyle?

Which of my current financial commitments feels like an obligation?

What feels like an opportunity?

How can I shift from obligation to opportunity?

When I'm 80, will I regret the risks I took with my money or the experiences I declined to preserve it?

What is the single best way I've ever spent money?

How can I make that type of impact a part of my financial decision-making framework?

What do I prioritize when things get tough?

What is the primary purpose of my wealth?

What do I need to achieve to be considered successful regardless of my net worth?

What's my vision for my finances for the next year?

What's my vision over the next five years?

What's my financial vision over the next ten years?

How do I envision my wealth over the next 20 years?

What's my physical clutter?

How does this clutter affect my finances?

If my physical clutter could talk to me, what would it say?

How can I declutter?

What action can I take to declutter *right now*?

What's my relationship clutter?

How does this clutter affect my finances?

If this relationship clutter could talk to me, what would it say?

How can I let go of relationships detrimental to my finances?

What action can I take *right now* to let go?

What is my health clutter?

How does this clutter affect my finances?

If this clutter could talk to me, what would it say?

How can I declutter?

What action can I take to declutter *right now*?

Who do I think is financially savvy?

Why do I think they are good with money?

What advice would I like to ask them?

Who doesn't have my best financial interests?

Why are they in my life?

What do I need to do so they don't affect my finances?

Who has my best financial interests?

How can they support me?

What's my debt?

How long have I been in debt?

Why am I in debt?

How much does the debt weigh on my mind?

How can I refinance or reduce my debt?

If my debt disappeared tomorrow, what's the first thing I'd do with my freed-up cash flow?

What do I need to pay "cash only" to ensure my debt doesn't return?

When I mindlessly spend money, what need am I trying to fulfill?

How can I healthily fulfill my needs?

What debt would I consider that could grow in value, such as a home or a degree?

How many hours of my life am I willing to go into debt for?

What action can I take *right now* to get out of debt?

What money am I owed?

Why haven't I been paid back?

How can I get the money I'm owed?

At one point, your physical clutter was money.

What do I need to consider when lending/giving money?

Who do I owe money to?

Why haven't I paid my debt(s)?

What's my plan to pay my debt(s)?

What do I need to consider when borrowing/asking for money?

What's my budget?

If I don't have a budget, why don't I?

What do I prefer for budgeting: paper, app, electronic, or a combination?

How well do I stick to my budget?

Where do I tend to overspend?

Why do I overspend?

How can I reduce overspending?

Where do I consistently adhere to my budget?

Why am I consistent in this area?

How can I apply my budgeting strengths to the areas where I struggle?

How often do I review my budget?

Am I fully aware of where all my money goes?

What do I need to do to improve my budget?

How does my financial clutter affect my intimate relationships?

How can I strengthen my financial situation to support these relationships?

How do my finances affect my friendships?

What can I do to improve my finances to foster healthier friendships?

How does my money management affect my family?

What financial strategies will help me positively impact my family?

How do my finances affect my work relationships?

What can I do to build financial stability that nurtures these relationships?

What are my investments?

How well do I understand my investments?

If I have a financial advisor, how happy am I with them?

How much have my investments and/or my advisor made me?

What are the fees/expense ratio?

How could I lose money in my investments?

What risk level am I most comfortable with?

What is my sleep well at night threshold for investing?

What would happen if my portfolio dropped 25% tomorrow?

Am I investing because of conviction or FOMO?

Your point of power is in the present moment .

Who uses my financial situation to make me feel "less than"?

Do I feel shamed by social media or societal "milestones" that suggest I should be further ahead than I am?

How can I respond when someone shames me about my finances?

Is the strongest voice of shame actually mine?

How can I ask for support from this person(s)?

Am I judging myself for past mistakes instead of focusing on today's potential?

How can I be more accepting of my financial struggles?

How can I acknowledge that I'm working to overcome my financial challenges?

Who in my life uses my financial struggles to make themselves feel superior?

How do I feel when they behave this way?

Who criticizes my money management?

Am I angry because they are wrong or because there is some truth in their criticism?

Do these people make me feel empowered to change or paralyzed by criticism?

Who competes with me financially?

Why do they want or need to compete?

How do I feel when someone competes with me?

How can I use this competition to my benefit?

Who do I try to compete with financially?

Why do I compete?

What's behind my need to compete about money?

How can I use competition to motivate myself?

What are my frivolous expenses?

How much do I spend on frivolous expenses monthly?

How many hours of work do these items cost me?

Why do I purchase frivolous items?

What am I giving up (saving for a vacation, retirement, etc.) when I purchase them?

What are my monthly recurring expenses (TV, gym, cable)?

Do I know the annual costs of each?

When was the last time I used them?

How can I reduce or eliminate these expenses?

What's my mental clutter?

How does this clutter affect my finances?

If my mental clutter could talk to me, what would it say?

How can I declutter my mind?

What action can I take to declutter *right now*?

What is my emotional clutter?

How does this clutter affect my finances?

If my emotional clutter could talk, what would it say?

How can I declutter my emotions?

What action can I take to declutter *right now*?

What is my spiritual clutter?

How does this clutter affect my finances?

If my spiritual clutter could talk, what would it say?

How can I declutter?

What action can I take to declutter *right now*?

What am I hiding from myself with my financial clutter?

What's the number I'm afraid to look at?

What's the lie I tell myself to purchase something I can't afford?

What envelope or app do I avoid opening?

Am I waiting to be rescued by something that may not happen (tax refund, inheritance, etc.)?

How do I sabotage my finances?

Why do I sabotage myself?

Do I feel guilty when I have more than my peers or family?

Do I "forget" to pay bills I have the money for?

True wealth isn't related to money; it's about living life fully.

Have I been waiting for the "perfect moment" to start clearing my financial clutter?

Do I skip easy wins (saving $10 vs. $1,000) because they feel too small?

Do I research excessively and delay decision-making to avoid acting?

Do I create financial drama to avoid the boredom of stability?

Do I suddenly have an emergency every time I reach a certain amount in savings?

How can I stop sabotaging my finances?

How much do I have in savings?

How much would I like to have saved in a year?

Where is it easy for me to save money?

When I got my last raise/bonus/tax refund, where did the money go?

How much would I like to have saved in 5 years?

How much would I like to have saved in 10 years?

How much would I like to have saved in 20 years?

What am I saving for?

If I lost my income tomorrow, how long before I'd panic?

What can motivate me to save?

What emergencies (pet, healthcare, job loss) should I prepare for?

Do I have a freedom fund so I can quit a toxic job, a bad living situation, etc.?

How much do I need to cover emergencies?

Can I easily access my money in a crisis?

How can I automatically save for an emergency to set and forget?

What's my timeline for achieving financial milestones (savings, debt-free, investing, etc.)?

What's my credit card debt?

How long have I had this debt?

How has my credit card debt changed over the past year: same, decreased, or increased?

Why did it stay the same or change?

What am I purchasing that creates credit card debt?

Why do I still buy things despite having debt?

What need am I trying to fulfill by buying things with money I don't have?

How can I better fulfill my needs?

How can I decrease my credit card debt?

What's my credit score?

How has my credit score affected me (interest/mortgage rates, etc.)?

What future purchases (car, home, etc.) do I need a good credit score for?

How can I improve my credit score?

What's my biggest opportunity *right now* to improve my finances?

How can I seize this opportunity?

Where am I frugal?

Why am I frugal?

Where am I too frugal?

How has being cheap affected my relationships?

When has being frugal cost me something?

How has being frugal supported me?

How can I balance being frugal and enjoying life?

What does financial success look like to me?

Am I chasing someone else's version of success?

Do I regularly check in on how I'm doing financially?

What's my financial fear?

What action can I take *right now* to face that fear?

What financial "mistakes" have I made?

Why did I make these "mistakes"?

Am I still punishing myself for my "mistakes"?

How can I forgive myself?

What's my plan if I slip up?

What financial issue am I procrastinating on?

Why am I procrastinating?

When do I deal with my money matters promptly?

Why do I deal with them promptly?

How can I apply my strengths to the areas where I struggle to respond promptly?

What can help me deal more directly with money matters?

Where am I losing money?

Do I regularly lose money, or was this a "one-off" like a freak accident?

Am I losing money because of a choice or a lack of action?

What guardrail was missing, and can I create one so I don't lose money again?

What money issue or situation keeps me stuck in the past?

Why does it keep me stuck?

How can I be more present with my finances?

What financial concerns propel me into the future?

Why do these financial issues concern me?

How can I be present to tackle these financial concerns?

The truth I don't want to admit about my money is:

Who in my life am I subsidizing that doesn't deserve it?

You are good enough, worthy enough, & loved no matter what.

Am I using money to control anyone?

Are my money problems really a discipline problem?

What do I need to know when hiring or firing a financial advisor?

What's important when someone else is managing my money?

What are my concerns with a financial advisor?

How can I address these concerns?

What are the benefits of having someone else manage my money?

Who am I comparing my finances to?

Why am I comparing?

Are they buying things I actually want, or am I jealous of their status?

What am I willing to trade for that lifestyle?

Am I comparing my behind-the-scenes with their highlight reel?

How can I use comparison for information to support my financial goals?

How abundant do I feel?

What makes me feel abundant?

How often to acknowledge and recognize my abundance?

What's my attitude towards money and wealth?

What was/is my family's attitude?

Are my beliefs mine or someone else's?

What are my negative beliefs about money and wealth?

What's my attitude towards rich people?

What's my family's attitude towards wealthy people?

Are my beliefs mine or someone else's?

What are my negative beliefs about wealthy people?

How well do I resolve financial conflicts in my intimate relationships?

How can I better resolve these disagreements?

How well do I resolve financial disputes with friends?

How can I better resolve these clashes?

How well do I resolve financial disagreements with family?

How can I better resolve these conflicts?

How well do I resolve financial differences at work?

How can I better resolve these conflicts?

What memory of not having enough still stings?

What memory of having plenty still comforts?

When I feel stressed or sad, does my spending go up or down?

What's my retirement plan?

How much do I have saved for retirement?

How long do I expect to work?

What's a realistic number I need to live comfortably in retirement?

What do I want to do in retirement?

What are my expected income sources in retirement?

How aggressively am I investing to achieve my goals?

How much will I depend on Social Security?

How much Social Security am I projected to have?

How many years do I need to plan for?

What's my plan to pay for healthcare in retirement?

How can I cover any long-term healthcare costs?

How much do I anticipate spending yearly?

What else do I need to consider when creating a plan for retirement?

When am I dishonest about financial matters in my intimate relationships?

How can I be more honest about money in these relationships?

How honest am I about my finances with my family?

How can I be more honest about money matters with my family?

When am I dishonest about money in my friendships?

How can I be more honest about money with my friends?

How honest am I about my finances at work?

Gratitude allows you to release clutter in all its forms.

How can I be more honest about my finances at work?

How well do I receive (compliments, gifts, etc.)?

When is it hard for me to receive?

Why is it hard for me to receive?

How can I be more receptive?

What finances make me anxious?

Why does this make me anxious?

How can I reduce my anxiety?

What aspects of finances (investing, budgeting) intimidate me?

Why do they intimidate me?

How can I gain confidence to deal with these issues?

When have I been taken advantage of financially?

How did I allow this to happen?

How did this make me feel?

How can I make sure I won't be taken advantage of again?

What purchase would I be most embarrassed to tell someone?

Why does this thing trigger shame?

Am I hiding financial infidelity from anyone?

What financial secrets am I keeping?

Why am I keeping secrets?

How can I resolve, or share, my secrets?

If I could wave a magic wand, what would be the first money problem I'd release?

What action can I take *right now* to tackle this problem?

What financial issue(s) make me feel powerless?

Why do they make me feel this way?

How can I feel more empowered about my finances?

When have I said yes to a financial request that I felt a no to in my gut?

What was I afraid would happen if I said no?

Am I'm buying my way out of guilt in any relationships?

Who makes me feel tight or anxious when they bring up money?

Is my financial help enabling someone's dysfunction?

Am I the family bank?

Do I have a gift limit, or do I let the occasion decide what I give?

How do I handle the "split the bill" moment?

How do my financial habits create physical clutter?

Do I have a peer pressure fund or blow my budget to keep up?

Am I working off the clock for free because I'm afraid to ask for the value of my time?

Can I say no without offering a long defensive explanation?

Does anyone have access to my financial details that they haven't earned?

Do I allow my future self to have a seat at the table?

What am I grateful for?

How often do I express my gratitude?

When am I ungrateful?

Why am I ungrateful?

How does my gratitude, or lack thereof, affect my finances?

Who makes me feel rich regardless of my bank balance?

What free experience(s) have I had that felt more valuable than a paid one?

What crisis from my past am I now grateful for because of the lesson it taught me?

How often do I pay it forward?

Why do I pay it forward?

Am I giving out of should or want?

Is my giving a secret or a statement?

What donation recently brought me the most joy?

Who helped me when they didn't have to?

How can I replicate that help for someone today?

What's currently my biggest financial challenge?

How can I see this challenge as an opportunity?

What action can I take *right now* to solve this challenge?

Who do I think is financially savvy?

Why do I think they are good with money?

What advice would I like to ask them?

How expensive is my home/living space to maintain?

Just because you've always done something doesn't mean you have to continue.

How can I reduce the cost of maintaining my living space?

What can I downsize (house, collections, clothes, etc.)?

What are my money habits?

When I'm bored, stressed, or celebrating, what's the first thing I spend money on?

Is my digital environment working against me (one-click purchase, etc.)?

Do I pay myself first or last?

What is a small habit that has a huge yearly total?

Who do I spend the most time with, and what are their money habits?

Does a “it’s on sale” mentality dictate my wants and needs?

How much estate planning have I done?

What insurance do I have?

When was the last time I reviewed my estate and/or insurance policies?

How can I celebrate clearing my financial clutter and acknowledge my work?

Look within for all the answers you seek.

ACTION PLAN: FINANCIAL CLUTTER

Here are some examples of what a decluttering plan may look like. Consider highlighting some of your answers to help you in creating a blueprint for action. Don't forget all that you'll gain from clearing your clutter. If you're feeling stuck, set a timer and see if you can complete one of your steps in 10 minutes. One foot in front of the other—keep on keeping on!

For the next month, I'm concentrating on budgeting. As I was answering the questions, I realized I have no clue how much I spend. Or save! I looked in my closet and wondered how many thousands of dollars I spent. Don't even ask me about purses!!! It's okay, though, I had an AHA moment and know I need to make changes. Once I outline my budget, I'm going to create a savings plan. I'm excited to get started!!!!

I realized doing these prompts that I'm more anxious about retirement than I realized. I have no clue how much I'll need and how to get there. I did email HR to see about our matching retirement plan so that made me less anxious. I have a good relationship with my boss, so I'm going to ask her advice. I also found a meditation app to listen to for stress. If I struggle a lot, I'll get professional help.

My BFF's mom died and she didn't make any plans for her pets. My BFF is completely stressed out as she can't have pets where she lives. I'd never want my babies thrown out on the street or end up in a shelter. I haven't slept all week thinking about it. I have written down all the things I think I need to do for estate planning. I'm talking with my cousin who is an estate planner next month as I'm sure there's a bunch of stuff I'm missing.

I know zero about investing. It intimidates me and all the information overwhelms me and make me scared to even try. I've done a little bit of research and came up with some companies to invest in. I'll ask for recommendations from family & friends for a financial advisor and within two weeks will contact three potential advisors.

I need to take baby steps so I don't become overwhelmed and quit. I'm going to:

- *Ask Shelley to help me find a budgeting app.*
- *Spend time contemplating my attitude towards wealth & wealthy people.*
- *Cancel my wine of the month subscription.*

Daily action creates change. 10 minutes a day adds up to 60 hours in a year.

MY TAKE ACTION PLAN: FINANCIAL CLUTTER

MY TAKE ACTION PLAN: FINANCIAL CLUTTER

IMMEDIATE TAKE ACTION PLAN

Perhaps you've completed just one section, accomplished half the questions, or answered every question and created a *Take Action* plan. No matter how much you've finished, you may be thinking, "Wow! I have a lot of clutter. Where do I start?" Even if you've sketched out items that need to be completed, you may be feeling overwhelmed. This next step is designed to help you shake off any paralysis when beginning your to-do list.

If you feel guided or believe that it might be supportive, go through your *Take Action* plan and highlight what's most urgent or that you feel moved to do *right now*. Record your tasks below. Refer to the beginning of the book for guidelines for making decisions and creating a successful strategy to accomplish your goals.

Concentrate on no more than three items as you begin the process of clearing your financial clutter.

Examples of what an *Immediate Take Action* plan may look like:

I figured out I don't trust my business partner with money. It's just a feeling, but I need to honor it. I'm meeting with our accountant next week to go over some numbers.

Answering a lot of these questions made me realize how I've been ignoring stuff. I have to focus that I've started. I'm still overwhelmed. My church has a financial literacy group and I've left a message for Rev. Paul to see if I can join. I'll have a baseline to start.

I discovered, or finally able to admit, that my relationship with Susan isn't healthy. I spend money I don't have when I'm with her and I drink a lot. I also started to notice she never really asks about my life and seems to call only when she needs money. I canceled Saturday night plans. Going to talk to my brother as he always has good advice.

Right now, all I can handle is downloading a budget app and starting to play around with it.

I need to take baby steps so I don't become overwhelmed and quit. I'm going to:

- *Write down what I purchased every day for two weeks.*
- *Talk to my BFF about my anxiety over not having much savings.*
- *Exercise four times a week to clear my head & think about how I can save money.*

MY IMMEDIATE TAKE ACTION PLAN

FINAL THOUGHTS

Whew! You did it! Take time to congratulate, honor, and reward yourself. Working through this journal took effort, awareness, courage, time, devotion, and commitment. I'm so proud of you! Take a moment to acknowledge all you've accomplished.

You've focused your energy by answering questions about financial clutter and have been guided to complete a *Take Action* plan. You might have also created an *Immediate Take Action* strategy based on what and where it's most important for you to begin decluttering.

I don't view this workbook as a "one and done." You might not have been able to answer all the questions, just completed one section, or know your circumstances are changing, and didn't answer some questions. Down the road, you might have very different responses and choose to go through all the questions again, complete a section you hadn't previously, or answer questions you skipped.

You now have a foundation of information to understand your financial challenges and a game plan to begin clearing your clutter. If you're unsure how to start, consider asking a trusted friend or getting professional support. There's no shame in seeking assistance, as it reminds you that you aren't alone, and we all benefit from giving and receiving care. I believe that when you ask for support and take that first step, the people who can help you show up in your life.

Life is about being in the present moment, and that is your point of power to change. Be in the flow of life and open to awareness, change, and discovery. Trust the process and know that you are exactly where you need to be.

I'm wishing you much love, happiness, peace, abundance, joy, and laughter.

Clear your clutter to create the life you choose, deserve, & desire.

RESOURCES

Clear Your Clutter Inside & Out Podcast & Videos are available on my YouTube channel, Seibert Radio. You can easily link to all my social media from my website, ReawakenYourBrilliance.com. Unfortunately, KDP did not allow links when I updated in 2026.

BOOKS, AFFIRMATIONS, MEDITATIONS, CLASSES & MORE

Find everything on my website, ReawakenYourBrilliance.com, in the shop section.

LET'S CONNECT

Go to my website to easily connect with me.

Facebook/ReawakenYourBrilliance

Instagram/reawakenyourbrilliance

LinkedIn/juliescoraccio

Need a more tailored approach to declutter your life?

Learn how Julie can support you in coaching, professional speaking, online workshops, & more.

ReawakenYourBrilliance.com

Gratitudes

I consciously used gratitudes because acknowledgements didn't fully capture how I truly felt.

To Tony, and our cats Joey, Antonio, Athena, Annina, and Augusta, for showing me daily that your love is all that matters. Tony, you're the best thing that ever happened to me by far. Joey, thanks for teaching mommy that cats are the best. Antonio, you let me know it would be okay, and Athena, mommy's girl with squeaky pipes and beautiful stripes. NiNi and Gus, I'm so glad you both rescued me.

Lisa Transcendence Brown, Judy Nelson, A. Kimball Pike, Mardi Wasserman, and all the other teachers along my path who have supported me in clearing my clutter.

My dear BFF Kaadi Taylor, thank you for being there when I needed you the most. I can never fully express what that meant to me. Thank you for all the writing projects you've read and given insightful feedback and suggestions to over the years. Your feedback for this book brought it to the next level. And, girl, your formatting skills are phenomenal.

To my father, James Seibert (Big J), who always believes in me and told me he would support me as long as I didn't do anything "illegal, immoral, or unethical."

My generous mother, Jenny Seibert (Jen Jen), for teaching me to always be kind, and to take the road less traveled, especially when traveling. Also, for reading and editing my first draft.

To my niece Emma for calling me out when I need it and making me my own *Varuit.*

For my nephew Max, for constantly teaching me that this is the best day ever.

To my niece Clare, who amazes me every time she dares to step on the stage.

My uncle, grammarian and fellow author, Jim Henry. You had invaluable insights.

For the *Clear Your Clutter Inside & Out* audience: thanks for listening and watching, and letting me know how much the episodes mean to you.

To my clients: You inspire me with your willingness to go deep and take risks. It's a lot easier to remain unaware, so Brava and Bravo!

For the readers undertaking the journey of this journal: the world desperately needs your gifts, so thank you for taking the first step to declutter your life.

Julie Coraccio lives in Wheeling, WV, with her husband, Tony, and their rescued black cats, Antonio & Jack Henry, and tuxedos NiNi & Gus. Joey, Athena, and Simon watch over everyone from the Rainbow Bridge.

A native West Virginian, she is passionate about supporting people in clearing clutter in all areas of their lives and becoming more mindful and aware. Julie is a graduate of Mount Holyoke College and hosted the popular weekly podcast *Clear Your Clutter Inside & Out.*

Julie enjoys hiking & playing tennis, cooking & baking, watercolor painting, alternative medicine & healing, supporting environmental and animal causes, and enjoying her woman cave—a bubble bath. Learn more at ReawakenYourBrilliance.com

Made in United States
North Haven, CT
05 November 2026

21763430R00122